WHY
Did I Do That?

A Comprehensive Look at
Why We Behave the Way We Do
and Who is Responsible for It

WHY Did I Do That?

A Comprehensive Look at Why We Behave the Way We Do and Who is Responsible for It

MIKE SIVER & APRIL SIVER
MAC, CDVC, BCBC

PUBLISHED BY FIDELI PUBLISHING INC.

©Copyrighted 2018, Mike Siver

All rights reserved.

Printed in the United States of America.

No part of this publication may be reproduced or transmitted in any form or by any means, electronic or mechanical, including photocopy recording, or any information storage and retrieval system without permission in writing from the publisher.

ISBN: 978-1-60414-780-3

MIKE SIVER
Business Center
49770 East Dr.
Decatur, MI 49045

Contact the atuthor at: Whydidi001@gmail.com

Cover art: © Can Stock Photo Inc. / davisales

Contents

Foreword .... *vii*

Expectations .... *xi*

CHAPTER 1
Why I Behave the Way I Do 1
    QUESTIONS 9

CHAPTER 2
The Sponge 13
    QUESTIONS 17

CHAPTER 3
The Early Years 21
    QUESTIONS 30

CHAPTER 4
Environmental Awareness vs. Environmental Conditioning© 35
    WHAT DOES THIS MEAN? 38
    HOW PARENTS CAN USE THIS CONDITIONING 38
    PUNISHMENT IN ENVIRONMENTAL CONDITIONING 39
    QUESTIONS 41

CHAPTER 5
Behavior/Belief or Belief/Behavior 45
    BEHAVIOR AND BELIEF OR BELIEF AND BEHAVIOR 46
    CHANGE YOUR BEHAVIOR 54
    QUESTIONS 56

CHAPTER 6

Try 59
- WHEN TRYING ISN'T ENOUGH 59
- POSITIVE USES 62
- NEGATIVE USES 62
- IMPLIED FAILURE 63
- SELF-FULFILLING PROPHECY 65
  - QUESTIONS 67

CHAPTER 7

We Teach People How to Treat Us 69
- PARENT FOLLOW THROUGH 70
- RESPECT FROM OUR PEERS 71
- ROMANTIC RELATIONSHIPS 72
- INTERACTIONS BETWEEN ADULTS 74
- CONCLUSION 75
  - QUESTIONS 75
  - AUTHOR'S NOTE 81

Performance Change 83
- PARENTING NONVIOLENTLY 83
- WHAT IT MEANS TO BE A PARENT 84
- SETTING LIMITS FOR CHILDREN 85

Exercises 86
- GUMBO 94
- FINGERTIP GOALS 95

CES-D Test for Depression 97

About the Author 105

Foreword

Fans, coworkers, friends, and anyone interested in a way to make someone's life a little better. My name is Pinklon Thomas and I'm writing the forward to this book for three reasons. First, because I enjoy the theory and philosophy that is displayed throughout the book, especially since I can relate to so much of it, based on my past personal experiences.

The second reason I support this book is that I support the efforts of the author, Mike Siver. Mike was introduced to me in April of 1993 as a co-worker. Through the years, we became partners in counseling, coaching and mentoring juvenile offenders at all levels — from minor first-time offenders to the repeat offenders of the most serious crimes. Mike and I worked closely together for many years, helping each other to help as many young people as we could.

My third reason to introduce this book is to support you, the reader. What is in this book will give you tools to help yourself or your loved ones through the difficult times that always come along.

I was fortunate in my life to be given great abilities, strength, and gifts from God. I have been able to use those gifts to help others find their way through difficult times. The individuals like Mike that surrounded me with support and encouragement played a big part in my success in these efforts.

My path to where I am now began when I was much younger. I realized I had a talent for boxing, and began fighting my way to the World Boxing Council, and the Heavy Weight World Championship in 1984. My great success was followed by personal failures and bad decisions. With determination, I found a way to learn from my past mistakes and realized that your blessings in life come from giving back. I took these lessons seriously, and today I have continued to overcome obstacles and have been on the right track for over 20 years.

As a result of my struggles, I created Project P.I.N.K. an acronym for Pride in Neighborhood Kids. This organization creates a better way for adolescents to set goals and dreams, and helps them to stay on the right track by guiding them to make good choices, and teaching them necessary skills such as proper etiquette, academics, and financial responsibility.

When I read Mike's book, my past flashed before my eyes, because as I said earlier, Mike and I go way back. I have seen Mike in action more times than I could count, and because of that, I know that what he put into this book is the real thing. The stories are real. The suggestions work. The failures will really happen just as he describes them if you keep doing what you are doing. He has been at this for years with hundreds of clients of all ages, and he remembers every one of them and he learned something from each experience. Much of it he has shared with us in his book.

Take a few minutes to scan through the chapters. I'm sure you will find something that gets your attention. No matter how well life seems to be going, we all have at least one area that we would benefit from a little work in. Many of us need a lot more work than others. Maybe this book will help you get started on your path to success.

Pinklon Thomas
WBC Heavyweight World Champion 1984–1986
IBO Heavyweight World Champion 1992

Expectations

I hope you find this book beneficial. I tried to cover information that would benefit individuals in a variety of life circumstances.

The stories I share are all actual experiences I have had with clients of all ages over the years. The overall purpose though is to teach you techniques to help you become the person you want to be. No matter where your life has led you up to this point, you can make a choice to improve it.

There are very few life settings that cannot be changed with the right decisions. Those decisions begin with deciding what you want to change, and then making changes, one behavior at a time.

— Mike Siver

CHAPTER 1

Why I Behave the Way I Do

*Change the way you look at things
and the things you look at change.*

~ WAYNE W. DYER

This book was written as a way to look at why we behave the way we do. My intent was to create a way of reaching more people with the message that there is hope to create the life you want, and also to try to provide some tools to help achieve that goal.

As a behavioral therapist, many people have asked me about my personal background over the years, and if I had personal experiences that led me to this profession. My response has typically been that, yes, I was a product of divorce and multiple childhood moves, but I usually left it there without elaboration.

It occurred to me that it might be beneficial to expand on my personal pathway through life as a way to help others on their journeys, as well as to help readers of this book relate better to me and to the message of the book.

I don't think what happened to me is much different from what happens to thousands of children each year. I went from a stable home life in a familiar place, to being uprooted and having my life turned upside down. While I'm sure my parents thought they were doing what was best for the family, they forgot to consider the impact this would have on each of their children's lives. And, each of my siblings reacted to and handled the moves differently.

This leads me to an important concept. Every individual sees the events of the moment through their own eyes. Because of this, when we start to evaluate who we are and how we became that way, we must stay focused on our perceptions of past events, and not try to analyze the actions of others.

I am one of seven children, all raised by the same mother, with five of us having the same father. If you gave all of us confidential questionnaires about events in our lives, we would each have different responses to most of the questions, even though we were participating in these events at the same time. As we grew up, we all developed different strengths and weaknesses. How can one of us blame our parents for a specific weakness when the rest of the children do not have that weakness?

The point is, this question has no answer and is irrelevant to the adult trying to improve his or her life. All that matters to our purpose of self-evaluation is *what we did* and *what we understood*. It will not help our cause to try to blame someone else. That will not change a thing.

> *Reject your sense of injury*
> *and the injury itself disappears.*
>
> ~ MARCUS AURELIUS

My personal worst childhood day is one I will never forget. I was about 11 years old and my parents were having trouble. They thought a fresh start might help, so they moved us from our lifelong home state of Michigan to a small town in Iowa, near an uncle and his family. As far as I knew, things were fine and I was trying to adjust to the new town and new school. After a few short months, I was starting to settle in.

One day at school, I went out to recess, assuming I would play a while and return to my desk. To my surprise, when I got outside I noticed my mother's car was parked alongside the playground and I heard her call my name. When I walked over to the car, all she said was, "Get in."

As always, I did as I was told. My siblings were already in the car, and she drove off with us all silently wondering what was going. What I thought about in those first few minutes was that my new friends would return to the classroom after recess and see I was gone. I wondered if they would think about where I had gone and if I was okay.

I don't remember anything else from that day, but I know we didn't stop driving until we were back in Michigan. I changed schools five times that year.

> ***If you keep on doing what you've always done, you'll keep on getting what you've always got.***
>
> ~ W.L. BATEMAN

That move was just one of many throughout my childhood years. We moved around enough that I always felt like the new kid in school. I also learned that as the new kid I could get away with a lot.

With each new school came the sympathetic teacher who made allowances for me academically because of the moves. As the new kid, I was usually popular because the other kids wanting to know about me.

It also seemed that as soon as the new kid image wore off, we would move again. In my mind, I was almost always the new kid and never had to try very hard to make friends or actually do my schoolwork. When I was 14, we finally settled in a small town and my mother decided the moving around would stop.

By the time I realized we weren't moving again, my grades were failing, I knew I was going to have to deal with this, but had no idea how. Actually doing the work and trying to learn the material never entered my mind. I did all I could do at school to distract from my failing grades.

I became one of those kids who was buddies with everyone, but friends with very few. I ran track, joined several after-school activities and excelled in them to draw attention to me and away from my grades. But, I was depressed all the time because no matter what I did, I was still failing my classes.

Worse still, I'd failed the fourth grade and was now in the same grade as my younger sister. So, when I had trouble in a class, the teacher would inevitably say something about having my sister help me or ask why I wasn't more like her. What I heard was, "Why aren't you as smart as your sister?"

The next move I made was to enlist in the US Navy at the age of 17. Although on its face, this seemed like a good move, joining the Navy was just another way of supporting my learned behavior of moving away from my problems.

I never thought about how the moves were impacting me at the time, but when I look back, I realize they did have a major impact on my efforts, my motivation, and most importantly on my ability to form meaningful relationships with others. I'm sure this is why I never really made any close friends. I used to have a hard time allowing friends to get close to me. I think in the back of my mind I believed they would be gone soon so there was no reason to make the effort.

Even though I am currently happily married to my third wife and am the father of three wonderful adult children, I have lived my entire life waiting for relationships to be taken away from me. Learning how to relax and trust others is a continuing effort for me.

As a behavioral therapist, I learned that I struggled with these insecurities and feelings earlier in life. As I went further

> ***The best way to find out if you can trust somebody is to trust them.***
>
> ~ ERNEST HEMINGWAY

into my studies, I found and learned ways of coming to terms with the losses I experienced as a child, such as the things I missed out on and the things I felt I was deprived of because of the frequent moves, i.e. stability, long-term relationships, a strong extended family, etc.

These are all important in the long term, but the important things to me then and to any child are the physical things, like toys. I don't remember how many toys I left behind as we moved around. As I got older and was in charge of my life, I had problems throwing anything away. It wasn't until after some education and understanding that I could start to let go of things I hadn't looked at for many years.

As I was educated as a therapist, I learned that I have strong insights. I will use these insights in groups and in this book to help you through your unique personal issues that are the root cause of many of the bad decisions you've made and continue to make. I am living proof that a bad start in life doesn't mean you have to end up with a bad life, and I will use my life experiences to help you understand the changes you need to make in your life.

> *We are taught you must blame your father, your sisters, your brothers, the school, the teachers — but never blame yourself. It's never your fault. But it's always your fault, because if you wanted to change you're the one who has got to change.*
>
> ~ KATHARINE HEPBURN

This chapter is not meant to place blame on my parents or yours, or your parenting style. It is not meant to make excuses. It is written in an effort to help you, the reader, understand me, the author, a little better so that I can help you to understand yourself a little better. All any of us can do is continue to learn and work on our ability to make decisions we understand and are proud of. It is an ongoing process.

As you read this book, please try to remember that your past is what made you who you are today, but it is also what placed you in some of the negative situations you find yourself in today.

Consider who you are and how you act today. Look for ways you can use experiences from your past and the information in this book to help take responsibility for your future actions so you can build the life you truly want. The road to your ideal life begins and ends with your decisions. Learn to make wise choices that benefit others, and you will be the one smiling.

> *The role we play changes with time and circumstances, and while we don't always have control over the role we are placed in, we do have control over the way we play it.*
>
> ~ MIKE SIVER

CHAPTER 1 QUESTIONS

Why I Behave the Way I Do

1. **Do you think your childhood was worse than that of most others?**

    ❏ Better

    ❏ About the Same

    ❏ Worse

    ❏ Much Worse

    Explain what you mean: _____
    _____
    _____

2. **What do you believe was your personal worst day while you were growing up?**

    Explain the day: _____
    _____
    _____

    Explain why it was the worst? _____
    _____
    _____
    _____
    _____
    _____

3. **From #2. How has it affected you in your adult life?**

   ❏ Positive

   ❏ Negative

   Explain why: _____

   _____

   _____

4. **What was the most memorable, positive event that happened in your childhood?**

   Explain the event: _____

   _____

   _____

   How did it affect you as you became an adult? _____

   _____

   _____

   _____

   Why did it have that effect? _____

   _____

   _____

   _____

5. Do you blame your parents or adult guardians for your problems today?

❑ Yes

❑ No

Explain why: _____

_____

_____

_____

6. Do you sometimes use your childhood experiences as a way to communicate, problem solve, and prioritize things as an adult?

❑ Yes

❑ No

❑ Still learning

Please explain: _____

_____

_____

_____

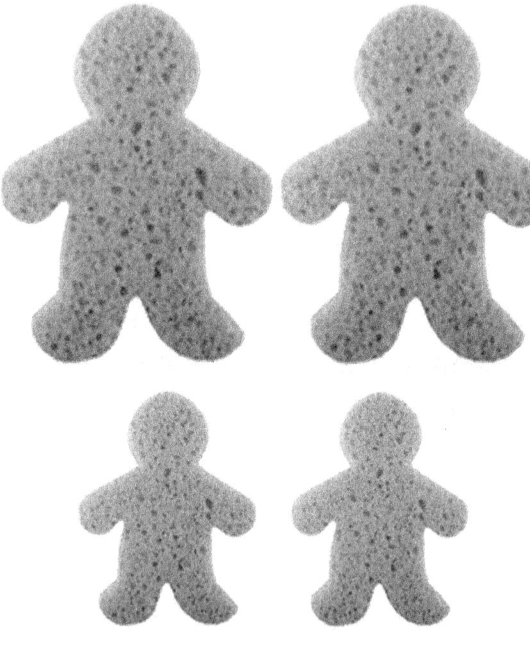

CHAPTER 2

The Sponge

*It is easier to build strong children
than to repair broken men.*

~ FREDERICK DOUGLASS

We all know children are like sponges — they mimic actions and repeat everything they hear, sometimes to our embarrassment. This is nothing most of us who have ever been around children for more than five minutes don't already know.

Children learn through the real activities and interactions of daily living. In other words, they learn how to act by watching the adults, teachers, and other children in their lives.

For example, a child who watches his father bully his mother might not automatically grow up to be a bully, but when he becomes a father, he will be more likely to bully his wife. That was the behavior he learned by watching his parents' interactions, so he will mimic that behavior when he finds himself in a similar situation.

Children soak up the behaviors they see as they grow up — both positive and negative. Those of us who were exposed to negative behaviors as children and find themselves repeatedly in bad situations must find a way to break the cycle and to learn how to wring out the old, negative behaviors and soak up some new, positive ones.

THE SPONGE©

For: Tuck, Haans, CJ, Mark, James, & David
From: A Father and Stepfather

When we are born we are like a new sponge. We are clean and empty. There is neither love nor hate.

A baby, like a sponge, has to stay in and absorb whatever is in the atmosphere in which he is living. If the atmosphere is full of love, support, kindness, honesty, fair play, ethical thinking, acceptance of others, etc., this is what he will absorb. If the atmosphere is full of hate, distrust, lying, drug or alcohol abuse, bigotry, racism, and selfishness, then this is what he will absorb.

We, like the sponge, will keep absorbing information until we are full. If what we absorb is love, kindness, honesty, fair play, ethical thinking and acceptance of others, then that is what we will give back to those around us. If, instead, we absorbed hate, distrust, lying, drug or alcohol abuse, bigotry, racism, and selfishness, then that is what we will give back.

Unlike a sponge, as we mature we can choose what we decide to absorb. If we find we are constantly in an atmosphere that forces us to absorb negative feelings and behaviors, then we must make a conscious effort to remove ourselves from that environment. Be prepared, this won't be easy because those who are perpetuating the negative will try to keep you there to absorb it.

> *The greatest power we have as a human being is to make a choice.*
>
> ~ MIKE SIVER

If you've started to wonder, "What role am I playing?" and decide it's time to make a change, you may find that drastic measures are necessary to get yourself out of the rut you're in. It could mean moving out of an unhealthy atmosphere, going to rehab, participating in individual or family counseling, or finding solace in religion. Think of these changes as wringing out the bad things that have been absorbed by your personal sponge. Once you've wrung them out, keep your sponge clean by absorbing positive energy and creating new behavior patterns.

This will not be an instant process. Just like a dirty sponge requires many rinses to be cleansed, you will probably need to make several passes before becoming completely successful in changing all of your behavior patterns. A person full of hate and distrust, who is used to lying and cheating, or taking drugs or alcohol, will have to work to keep from slipping back into old patterns. This is where the need for consistent support is the strongest. Do not feel you must achieve this change all on your own. Seek support from professionals like therapists and pastors.

Changes must be accompanied by love and understanding combined with a lot of education. The education isn't just for the individual, but should also include his or her family and friends.

Everyone involved in your life and your journey to change must be on the same page, or you will not be successful. Keep communication open with family and friends and allow them to provide the support you need to find success. Doing this will let you to achieve the goal you've set for yourself, and allow you to break out of the mold that was set for you in childhood. Once you've done that, you can become a responsible, productive person who is proud of the role he is playing in his life.

> *Live so that when your children and others think of fairness, truth, caring and integrity, they think of you.*
>
> ~ MIKE SIVER

CHAPTER 2 QUESTIONS

Sponge

1. **What was your sponge filled with when you were a child? Describe what you mean.**

   ❑ Good: _____
   _____
   _____

   ❑ Bad: _____
   _____
   _____

   ❑ Fun: _____
   _____
   _____

   ❑ Scary: _____
   _____
   _____

   ❑ Love: _____
   _____
   _____

   ❑ Hate: _____
   _____
   _____

2. **Do you need to wring anything out of your sponge?**

   What? _____

   _____

   How will you do it? _____

   _____

   _____

   Will you need help to wring out your sponge?_____

   What will you replace it with? _____

   _____

   _____

3. **If you have children, describe what you have filled their sponges with so far?**

   ❏ Good

   ❏ Bad

   ❏ Fun

   ❏ Scary

   ❏ Love

   ❏ Hate

4. **Do you believe you need to make some changes to make sure your children's sponges are positive and healthy?**

   ❑ Yes

   ❑ No

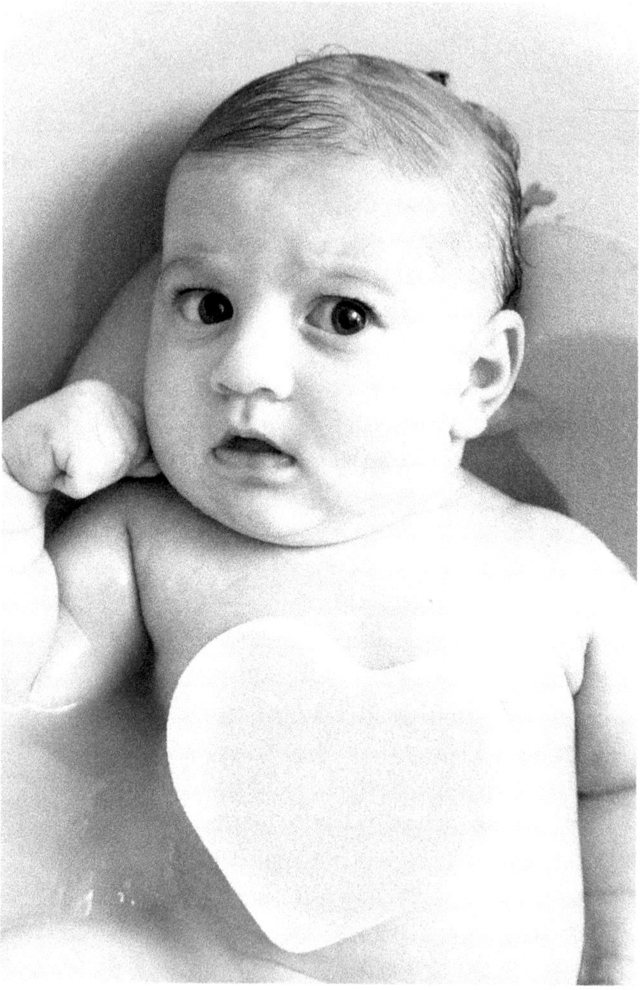

CHAPTER 3

The Early Years

The thing about family disasters is you never have to wait long before the next one puts the previous one into perspective.

~ ROBERT BRAULT,

As discussed in Chapter 2, children see, hear, and absorb everything that goes on around them. In many cases, it can be humorous, like cussing at the dog for making a mess in the house the way Dad does. Other times, it can be a little frightening, like a five-year-old using a knife in an electrical outlet the way he's seen Dad use a screwdriver on his bicycle.

By the time children become adults, most of this type of inappropriate behavior will be gone, or at least under control. Unfortunately, another type of learning that involves how children learn to act based upon what they see the adults in their life doing says with us into adulthood. This is officially called Environmental Situational Learning.

This powerful type of learning becomes imbedded a child's mind and shapes how he or she interacts with others throughout life. Typically by age 10, children have observed and absorbed all they need to know about how to act as adults. The behaviors of their parents, relatives, teachers, influential friends, and other people they see as authority figures help to shape how they will deal with life as an adult.

On the following pages are two examples of what might occur in an American home today, and how the behaviors of the people involved could be absorbed by children. These scenarios show how careful adults should be when interacting with children, as well as illustrating how some adult behaviors are grounded in what we were exposed to when we were children.

> *Have a heart that never hardens, a temper that never tires, a touch that never hurts*
>
> ~ CHARLES DICKENS

The Early Years

SCENE # 1

Dad sits in front of the TV, drinking beer and watching the Saturday football game with some friends. The child sees Dad watching the game, and notices Mom often gets chips, dip and beer for Dad, and maybe his friends as well.

After Dad has had too much to drink, he stops *asking* Mom to bring him things, and starts *demanding* instead. He might also grab or push her if he decided she's not doing things quickly enough to suit him.

The next morning there is an argument about the way Dad acted, and the things he said and did. Two things could happen as a result of this argument:

1. Dad will becomes apologetic and says it will never happen again, with Mom responding that she will leave him if it does because this is not the way she wants her children to grow up.

2. Dad will get defensive and tell Mom this activity is the one thing he likes to do with his only free time, and if she doesn't like it she can leave his house and take the children with her.

What the children absorb in either instance would not be good. The children have seen their father treating their mother badly, including verbal and physical abuse. They've also seen their parents argue and threaten each other with ultimatums that will impact them negatively.

Had this scene been Dad enjoying watching television and having snacks and a beer, the information the child would absorb would've been completely different. The message learned would've been that when the game is on, Dad gets a beer, stops whatever he's doing and watches the game. Sometimes, Mom might watch it with him, too.

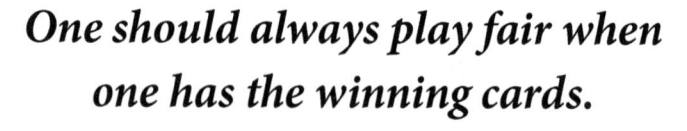

> *One should always play fair when one has the winning cards.*
>
> ~ OSCAR WILDE

SCENE # 2

Mom and Dad both work to keep the household running smoothly. On payday, Dad stops on the way home to meet with friends and have a few beers. Dad comes home late and Mom is upset because the children went to bed without seeing him, and the work she put into his evening meal is wasted. On top of that, he's spent money needed to pay the family's bills.

Dad feels his authority is being challenged and acts as if he should be able to do whatever he wants with the money he earns. He doesn't want to accept the fact that he acted irresponsibly. Mom is disappointed and hurt by Dad's lack of maturity and selfish attitude.

This is the point where some men become physical if they haven't learned the skills necessary to deal with anger and confrontation. They cannot deal with someone, in this case a spouse, questioning their behavior, motivation, maturity, etc.

and react with violence to vent their frustration. This reaction is most likely based on what was learned from the behavior of the adults in his life during his childhood.

Unfortunately, he is passing this learned behavior on to his children as they watch and listen to his interaction with their mother. Because parents are the ultimate authority figures in children's lives, they think the way their parents behave is the way things should be. They absorb that information and carry it with them into their adult lives, where they will most likely exhibit the same behavior when faced with a similar situation.

> *Don't judge each day by the harvest you reap but by the seeds that you plant.*
>
> ~ ROBERT LOUIS STEVENSON

Environmental Situational Learning comes into play when children see parents and authority figures in their lives behave in specific ways, at specific times, and in specific situations. If these behaviors are repeated often, the child not only learns the behavior and when to act that way, but also what role they're playing in life, i.e. mother, father, teacher, to match the actions.

As children become teenagers, they're more likely to emulate behaviors of their friends and those in their peer group they consider popular, rather than the adults in their lives. The things learned at this time, along with the behaviors learned from adults during their early childhood will coalesce in adulthood and form the background for the person's behavior patterns.

Many times, the true picture of the person's behavior won't emerge until marriage. Behavior that was fine with buddies and dates, will not be acceptable after marriage and this can trigger behavior learned in the childhood home. For example, the male child who grew up with the parents from Scene 2 would assume that getting drunk in front of the TV and disrespecting his wife is how marriage works and how he should behave.

The real problem in this case is the man is playing the role a husband would play and he's playing it the way he thinks it should be played because that is the way he saw it being done when he was growing up. This is the Environmental Situational Learning at work.

Females are not exempt from this, either. A young girl who sees her mother working hard to make a home —only to be yelled at by her husband, and possibly physically abused by him — will accept this type of behavior from her husband. She has perceived it is a woman's lot in life to put up with this type of behavior from

> **The only way you may correct the bad things in your past is to add better things to your future.**
>
> ~ SHILOH MORRISON

her husband. Children grow up to become a husband/dad or wife/mother who acts just like their parents did in those roles. No matter what the scenario, if children observe negative behaviors in their home environment, they will absorb them and when they are in a similar situation as an adult they will act as they learned.

Many times what we try to teach our children through our words is not the same as what we allow them to witness through our actions. No matter what parents tell their children, what they see in the home on a daily basis is what becomes ingrained in their minds and will influence their behaviors as they move on to adulthood.

The opposite end of the scale is when children are brought up in a home where parents are loving and exhibit positive behavior. Children who grow up in this environment have boundaries and learn from watching healthy relationships. They experience situational learning that is positive and loving, and this is what they carry into their adult lives and ultimately impart to their own children. These families are full of strong, emotionally healthy people.

Don't despair if your childhood is more like Scene 1 or 2 than you'd like to admit. You've already taken the first step toward change by acknowledging your behavior isn't what it should be. Next, you need to develop the confidence, courage, and commitment to change and then try a new, better behavior to replace the old one. Cultivate a loving and supportive environment so that your new behavior can flower and grow. You *can* change your learned behavior, but be aware that it will take time and effort on your part and cooperation and support from the people in your life.

> *I thought growing up was something that happened automatically as you got older. But it turns out it's something you have to choose to do.*
>
> ~ FROM THE TELEVISION SHOW SCRUBS

CHAPTER 3 QUESTIONS

The Early Years

1. **Do you have a behavior that got you into trouble with adults when you were a child, and sometimes still does now that you're an adult?**

    ❏ Yes

    ❏ No

    ❏ Please describe: _____
    _____
    _____

2. **How does the behavior displayed in Scene #1 of this chapter relate to you today?**

    ❏ It doesn't

    ❏ Only a little

    ❏ It's me

    Describe what you mean: _____
    _____
    _____

3. **Does the situation in Scene #2 remind you of your youth? Do you still have those kinds of thoughts if you are a provider?**

   ❏ Yes

   ❏ No

   ❏ Sometimes

   ❏ Please explain: _____
   _____
   _____

4. **Did you act a certain way while you were dating, and then change after you were married?**

   ❏ Yes

   ❏ No

   ❏ Please explain: _____
   _____
   _____

   Why did you change? _____
   _____
   _____

5. **If you have children, did you/are you raising them in a way that goes against what you said you were going to do when you grew up?**

   ❏ Yes

   ❏ No

   Explain what you are doing differently: _____
   _____
   _____
   _____

   Why did you change your plans? _____
   _____
   _____
   _____

6. **Have you been told your words do not reflect your actions?**

   ❑ Yes

   ❑ No

   ❑ Sometimes

   Please give an example: _____
   _____
   _____
   _____

   Explain why your words and actions are or are not the same: _____
   _____
   _____
   _____

Your Life

Your Environment

The Future of that Environment

What role do you play?

CHAPTER 4

Environmental Awareness vs. Environmental Conditioning©

Nobody has ever before asked the nuclear family to live all by itself in a box the way we do. With no relatives, no support, we've put it in an impossible situation.

~ MARGARET MEAD

Two friends, an environmentalist and a counselor, were talking about being environmentally aware, and how important it is for the kids of today to be exposed to this idea. If they learn to protect the environment, the environment can then survive, which will, in turn, allow the children of today and generations to come to also survive.

The environmental activist and juvenile counselor both understood that overcrowding and poverty in our large cities creates an environment that needs to be addressed, but they each approached the problem in different ways.

The environmentalist was worried about the trees, grass, and vital things of nature we're losing on a daily basis. She believed that if our youth weren't involved in efforts to reverse this trend, then there might come a time when the environment could not recover.

The counselor completely agreed with her, but he was more concerned with looking at the environments youth live in. He told her the youth he worked with were more worried about surviving in their community environment than about the earth's environmental issues.

The counselor elaborated, saying that as far as the long-term big picture for the earth's future was concerned, he agreed that all of us need to be more environmentally aware. He also stressed that this awareness needed to go hand in hand with environmental conditioning — being aware of your surroundings and what it takes to survive in them. He was adamant that this was extremely important for today's youth. He illustrated his point with the following story.

Chad sat on his front porch watching a vehicle drive by slowly, as if it were on the prowl. He watched it go off into the distance, stop, and then slowly turn around and head back in his direction. Inch by inch, it came toward him, picking up speed as it went. As it drew up even with is house, two of the three occupants rolled down their windows and opened fire.

Luckily for him, the boy was aware of his environment because he has grown up with an acute sense of self-preservation. His gut feeling was that something wasn't right, so by the time the car was near his home, he was already moving off the porch and on his way around the side of the house. His environmental conditioning saved his life.

The two friends continued talking and moved on to discuss young animals in the wild, and how they are taught by their parents. They learn to stay close with other young, and they all learn the same kind of survival techniques for their environment. They know they can only protect each other more easily by staying in groups and presenting the image that they're larger and more powerful.

The dynamic in neighborhoods works much the same way for young people. The term "safety in numbers" is true and a survival technique. What we sometimes forget, though, is that we have the ability to change our environment by moving somewhere safer.

The counselor explained that in the wild, pure animal instinct motivates the animal parents to start teaching their youngsters survival techniques as soon as they are born. Unfortunately, humans don't always teach their young environmental awareness and the children are left to fend for themselves.

> *Call it a clan, call it a network, call it a tribe, call it a family. Whatever you call it, whoever you are, you need one.*
>
> ~ JANE HOWARD

What does this mean?

The examples in the two discussions are dealing with operant or environmental conditioning, which plays a powerful role in everyday learning. Reinforcement and punishment take place almost every day in natural settings, classrooms, and therapy sessions. Behaviorist B.F. Skinner believed we should look only at the external, observable causes of human behavior, rather than looking at internal thoughts and motivations.

Skinner studied how the consequences of people's actions influenced their behavior. He used the term "operant" to refer to any active behavior that *operates* upon the environment to generate consequences. In other words, his theory explained how we acquire the range of learned behaviors we exhibit each and every day.

This conditioning relies on a fairly simple premise — actions that are followed by reinforcement will be strengthened and more likely to occur again. For example, if a student raises his hand and asks a question, and earns praise from the teacher for his polite behavior, then he will be more likely to raise his hand the next time he has a question or comment. Because the behavior was followed by a desirable outcome, the desire to repeat the action is strengthened. In the same way, actions that result in punishment or undesirable consequences will be weakened and are less likely to occur again.

How parents can use this conditioning

Positive reinforcement encourages good behavior. This reinforcement can be strengthened by the addition of something, such as praise or a direct reward, to encourage future good behavior. For example, if a child does a good job completing his chores for the week, the parents gives him a small reward for the good behavior to encourage a repeat of that behavior.

Negative reinforcement encourages bad behavior. In these situations, a response is strengthened by the removal of something considered unpleasant. For example, if a child starts to scream in the middle of the grocery store, but stops once the parent gives him a treat. Next time the child starts to scream, the parent will be more likely to give him a treat in an effort to stop the screaming. The action of giving a treat led to the removal of the unpleasant condition (the child screaming), but negatively reinforced this behavior by showing the child he will get a reward for screaming.

In both of these cases of reinforcement, the behavior increases because a rewards was provided in response to the behavior.

Punishment in Environmental Conditioning

Punishment is an adverse event or outcome that causes a decrease in the behavior it follows. In other words, you do something bad and you are punished for that behavior. There are two kinds of punishment:

Positive punishment, sometimes referred to as punishment by application, presents an unfavorable event or outcome in order to weaken the response it follows. An example would be spanking for misbehavior.

Negative punishment, also known as punishment by removal, occurs when a favorable event or outcome is removed after a behavior occurs. For example, taking away a child's video game following misbehavior.

In both cases, the behavior decreases in order to avoid the negative consequence.

Parents, guardians, teachers and other authority figures in children's lives should be the ones to consistently provide both positive reinforcement of good behaviors and punishment for negative behaviors. A young person who grows up in an environment with the understanding that when he or she makes a choice, he or she will be held accountable for that choice is a young person who will live a responsible life.

As parents, you need to ask yourselves: What role do I play in supporting my children and helping them understand the role they play in their lives, in their environment, and in the future of that environment? Teaching children right from wrong, good behavior from bad, and how to survive in the environment where they live goes a long way toward ensuring they become responsible, productive adults who care about their children, their community, their fellow man and the earth's environment.

> *I am the master of my fate:*
> *I am the captain of my soul.*
>
> ~ WILLIAM ERNEST HENLEY

CHAPTER 4 QUESTIONS

Environmental

1. **Do you think too much time and energy is spent on the worldwide environment and not enough on individual quality of life within your own community/environment?**

   ❏ Yes

   ❏ No

   Explain: _____
   _____
   _____

2. **Are you so caught up "just making it" that you are losing sight of your role in both of your environments?**

   ❏ Yes

   ❏ No

   Explain: _____
   _____

   If you think you should change, how will you do it?_____
   _____
   _____

3. **Do you believe you are a product of your individual environment, and therefore are unable to make any changes?**

   ❏ Yes

   ❏ No

   Explain: _____
   _____

   Is there anything you can do to change things? _____
   _____
   _____

4. **Do you believe your personal environment is a product of attitudes & acceptances like "that's just the way it is"?**

   ❏ Yes

   ❏ No

   Explain why you do/do not think that: _____
   _____
   _____

   Explain why you think this is/is not that way: _____
   _____
   _____

What could you do to make a change for yourself?

_____
_____
_____
_____
_____

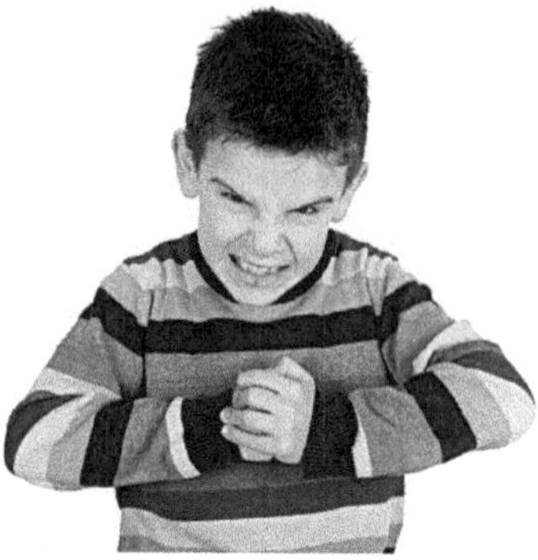

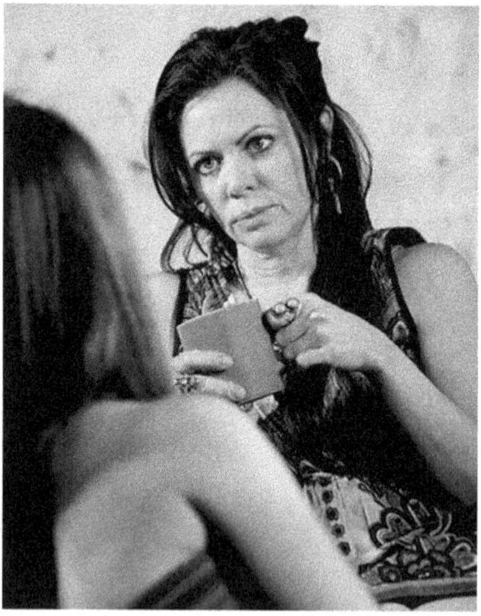

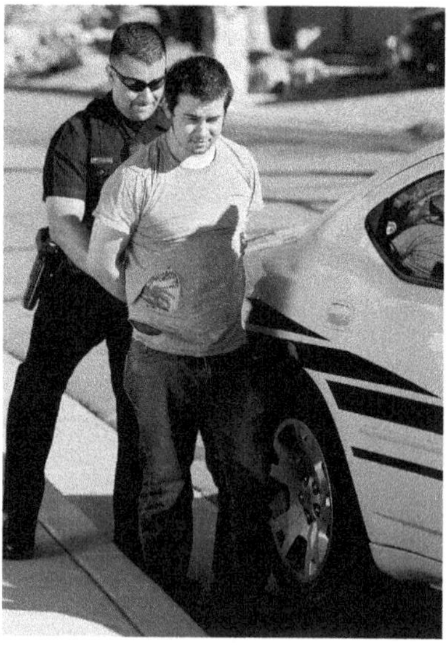

CHAPTER 5

Behavior/Belief or Belief/Behavior

*If you don't like how things are, change it!
You're not a tree.*

~ JIM ROHN

When we are born, our behaviors create our first beliefs. Later on, our beliefs create our behaviors. Those behaviors will be both positive and negative, but when the negative behaviors start to have serious consequences, it is time to evaluate our belief system.

Sometimes, it is difficult for us to understand that our initial belief system is created by our early behavior system. As we get older, it can become difficult for us to understand that our behavior system is created from our belief system, and if we change our belief system it will change our behaviors. When our behaviors stop getting us what we want and start getting us into trouble, it is then that we become motivated to change our belief system and create new behaviors that are more positive and productive.

> *Remember, if you're headed in the wrong direction, God allows U-turns!*
>
> ~ ALLISON GAPPA BOTTKE

BEHAVIOR AND BELIEF OR BELIEF AND BEHAVIOR

As stated above, your behaviors are a result of your belief system. The following stories come from the common threads found repeatedly in their counseling and coaching experiences. These stories combine elements of dozens of sessions conducted by the counselors. They are included here in an attempt to illustrate the critical relationship between our beliefs and our behaviors.

When we are young we learn and clearly understand it is our behavior that gets us the things we need (changed, fed and comfort). In this instance, this behavior and expectation are acceptable, because this is the only effective way the very young can communicate.

As we get older, we learn which additional behaviors get us what we need. We also learn and believe that various behaviors will *always* get us not only what we need, but also what we want. This is where a problem can start, because…

Your behavior creates your belief.

OUR BEHAVIOR HAS BECOME OUR BELIEF.

EXAMPLE 1: THE CHILD

Barry grew up with everything a young person could ever need or want. He was a normal child in the beginning, acting out with the typical behaviors to make sure he was fed, changed, and made comfortable. The problems began when he didn't stop these behaviors as he got older. He became a spoiled child, who was preoccupied by thoughts of what he didn't have, He lacked discipline and never learned he had to earn the things he wanted.

If he wanted something and his parents wouldn't give it to him, he thought all he had to do was act out or make more noise and suddenly it would be his. His parents indulged him, and this is how he came to believe he could get what he wanted through bad behavior. The older he got, the worse this became. Now, in order to get what he wants, his bad behavior has escalated to intimidation and even violence.

His behavior starts to get him into trouble outside of his home, but his parents bail him out each time, reinforcing his belief that it doesn't matter what he does, he will always get what he wants in the end.

As this cycle progresses, worse and worse behavior is required to continue to get what he needs. He actually plans manipulative scenes with his parents to ensure he gets his way. He understands there will be consequences for these actions, but he learns to accept them because even with the maximum consequences, he still wins in the end.

At this point, his behavior is pretty much out of control, and controls his household. He wonders why his parents don't trust him and don't like to be around him much. He calls them distant parents and blames them for his problems, but never asks himself what role he's playing in all of this. Because he's never been denied when he exhibits bad behavior, he has no idea that what he's doing is ultimately destructive to himself and his family.

> *Most of the shadows in this life are caused by our standing in our own sunshine.*
>
> ~ RALPH WALDO EMERSON
> OUR BEHAVIOR HAS BECOME OUR BELIEF.

EXAMPLE 2: THE ADULT

Mary borrows money from Janice and says she'll pay it back on payday. Her friend expects this will happen because she believes Mary, and it's a reasonable expectation.

Come payday Mary doesn't pay Janice back. Instead, she gives her several excuses why she can't repaying her and assumes this is okay. Then later, she tells her friend her family is going to an expensive amusement park that weekend because they need to relieve some stress.

Mary hasn't considered whether her friend had to sacrifice something in order to loan her the money. She also doesn't know if her friend desperately needed the repayment to pay her bills, buy groceries, etc. Mary is only concerned with herself and her happiness.

Janice was there for her in her time of need, but Mary is unwilling to make a sacrifice to repay her. Instead, she wants to go do something fun with her family because she believes this is more important. Mary believes others should understand her behavior and how important things are to her and that this bad behavior should cause her no consequences.

No action is without consequence. By behaving selfishly Mary might have some fun and receive instant gratification, but she will probably lose a friendship. At the least, this friend will not loan her money again. She might not even want to be Mary's friend after this incident.

> *If you think only of yourself, if you forget the rights and well-being of others, or, worse still, if you exploit others, ultimately you will lose. You will have no friends who will show concern for your well-being. ... By contrast, if an individual is compassionate and altruistic, and has the interests of others in mind, then irrespective of whether that person knows a lot of people ... he or she will immediately make friends. And when that person faces a tragedy, there will be plenty of people who will come to help.*
>
> ~ DALAI LAMA

OUR BEHAVIOR HAS BECOME OUR BELIEF.

EXAMPLE #3

Jeff is a seasoned tradesman who takes care of his responsibilities, but he also believes his behavior is always acceptable if no harm is done. One Friday evening, as he's leaving work, he realizes he needs of one of the tools from his work site to complete a project at home. His belief is that there is no harm done if he borrows it for the weekend and returns it on Monday morning, so he loads it into his car and heads home.

On Monday morning, Jeff is late getting to work, so he decides to leave the borrowed tool in the back seat of his vehicle until he can return it after everyone leaves for the day. When he walks onto the work site, he finds his boss speaking with a police officer about the missing tool. He avoids them and gets right to work, hoping no one will question him.

Later in the day, he's called to the boss's office. A policeman is there when he enters the office, and asks for Jeff's car keys.

The policeman recovers the tool from Jeff's car, and Jeff soon finds himself in handcuffs in the back of a police car.

This time, Jeff's behavior has resulted in being arrested and losing good-paying job. He found himself in a situation where his reasoning didn't work and no one would listen to his excuses. They didn't care that he *believed* it was okay to "borrow" a tool from his workplace.

For the first time in his life, Jeff finds himself seriously questioning his belief system. The lesson that actions have consequences has hit home for him in a big way, and he starts to realize he needs to make some changes so he won't find himself in this situation again.

> *Face what you think you believe and you will be surprised.*
>
> ~WILLIAM HALE WHITE

CHANGE YOUR BEHAVIOR

Barry, Mary and Jeff found out in the previous stories, the only way to change your behavior is to change your belief system.

They need to work through the stages of behavior change to turn their lives around. The stages include:

1. Precontemplation. In this stage individuals are not aware they have a problem. They engage in bad and risky behaviors for many reasons, but the main one is that they work in the short term. In the long term, they can have devastating consequences, ruin lives and even prove fatal.

2. Contemplation. In this stage it may occur to the individual that they actually have a problem, as happened in the story with Jeff. Suddenly, their behaviors are resulting in unexpected consequences, like others taking notice, health problems or run-ins with the law.

3. Preparation for Action. In this stage the individual acknowledges and accepts the fact that their behavior is a problem and are considering what to do about it. Now is the time when the individual can benefit from information about counseling, treatment for drug or alcohol abuse, or mental health issues.

4. Action. In this stage the individual takes action, which can take various forms including going for counselling, seeking help for addiction, etc. It can also be helpful for people to change certain elements in their environment to foster success. This may include moving to a new neighborhood and cutting ties with friends who are bad influences. This is because misery loves company and people will try to pull their friends back down to their low level. At this stage individuals may not be fully prepared to commit. They may still be waffling back and forth.

Once you realize you no longer believe the old behaviors will work for you, you'll find that you have the desire to create some new beliefs and behaviors. Just be sure that your new beliefs guarantee your integrity and truthfulness and are not based on self-centered thoughts and desires.

When your new beliefs begin influencing your behaviors, you will see positive changes in your life. The way those around you respond to you will also change because they can trust you to do the right thing. If you desire to be a person of ethics and integrity, then your behavior will reflect this. A possible benefit to these changes is that time spent with your family and others will suddenly become *quality* time. Once you have integrated these into your life, you can start to hand this better behavior down to your children so that they can eventually pass on traits of trust and ethical behavior to their offspring.

> *Seek freedom and become captive of your desires. Seek discipline and find your liberty.*
>
> ~ FRANK HERBERT

CHAPTER 5 QUESTIONS

Behavior/Belief

1. **Are there behaviors you used as a child that might still work for you today?**

    ❏ Yes

    ❏ No

    Explain the behaviors: _____
    _____

    Do you use them today? Why or why not: _____
    _____
    _____

2. **Are there behaviors or beliefs you used as a child that you see *do not* work in your adult life and you have been forced to change them?**

    ❏ Yes

    ❏ No

    Explain: _____
    _____
    _____

3. **Of the behaviors you believe work for you as an adult, are there any you remember using as a child?**

   ❏ None

   ❏ A few

   ❏ A lot

   Explain: _____
   _____

4. **Does the story in Example #1 relate to you or anyone you know? Do you feel this behavior is a concern today?**

   ❏ Yes

   ❏ No

   Explain: _____
   _____

5. **Is a feeling of entitlement part of your belief system today?**

   ❏ Yes

   ❏ No

   Explain why or why not: _____
   _____
   _____

6. **As described in Example # 2, do you feel people should understand and make allowances for you when you aren't able to live up to your obligations?**

   ❑ Yes

   ❑ No

   Explain: _____

   _____

7. **When considering the story in Example #3, do you believe that you should or should not get into trouble for doing something like this?**

   ❑ Yes

   ❑ No

   Explain: _____

   _____

CHAPTER 6

Try

Pick battles big enough to matter, small enough to win.

~ JONATHAN KOZEL

When someone says something like, "Oh, I've tried so hard to quit smoking and I just can't seem to quit," or "I've tried so many different diets and none of them work," do you wonder if they believe they're really going to be successful?

At what point in our lives did we learn and accept that trying as hard as we think we can and quitting is okay? The following pages will help all of us understand why merely trying can go hand in hand with failure.

WHEN TRYING ISN'T ENOUGH

"I'll try it, and do the best I can." How many times have you heard someone say that? Society today has made people think they'll be rewarded or not penalized as long as they're trying. People who grew up with parents who rewarded their effort rather than their actual success have problems as adults, because in the real world trying without succeeding is not enough.

When mediating anger management and substance abuse groups as well as family therapy, especially when young people are involved, it is common to hear these phrases often: "I'm *trying* to change." "I'm *trying* to understand, but I just can't." They expect to be rewarded for trying, but have no real commitment to change or understand the situation. Learning that trying isn't enough is a tough lesson to learn, but it must be learned before finding success in life. Those who don't learn, are destined to fail and will have a difficult time understanding why.

On the following is the definition of the word Try. Please read it completely, as knowing the definition will serve as a foundation for the rest of this chapter.

> *The essential question is not, "How busy are you?" but "What are you busy at?"*
>
> ~ OPRAH WINFREY

try

trī

verb

try\tried\ trying

1. a. to examine or investigate judicially
   b. to conduct the trial of;

2. a. to put to test or trial;
   b. to test the limit or breaking point: STRAIN (try one's patience)

3. to melt down and obtain in a pure state: RENDER (try lard from pork fat)

4. to make an attempt: ENDEAVOR [from Old French, "to pick out, sift"].

*Synonym—ATTEMPT, STRIVE: TRY suggests effort to experiment made in hope of determining facts, or of testing or proving something (tried various occupations);

Attempt: suggests a beginning of or venturing upon something and often implies failure (attempted to break through the enemy lines);

Strive: implies effort (strive to achieve lasting peace)—try one's hand: to attempt something for the first time.

Source: Webster's School Dictionary

The following pages are intended to help you understand why you believe "trying" to do something is good enough. It will also highlight when this likely stopped working for you and why it was hard for you to understand.

POSITIVE USES

Try is used when organizations or individuals want to create something new, or take something that has already been built and make it do something different. In both cases, you try it once, and then work on it until it's complete. Here are some examples of appropriate uses for the word try:

Professional:

Legal: "How will we try the case?"

Medical: "We need to try something."

Business: "Let's try to buy that company."

Management: "Would you try to see if you can make this thing better?" or "This tool doesn't do what I want, so let's try to find a better one."

Personal:

"Let's try to climb that wall."

"I'm going to try and redo this with fewer parts in less time."

"If we try hard, we will finish the housework before noon."

"We can win the game next week if we try a little harder."

All of these uses are positive, and the word "try" implies motivation. When used, in this context, the word try generates action, teamwork, and energy.

NEGATIVE USES

The word try is often used as a way to seem to be accomplishing something but have an excuse for not completing it. Here are some examples.

Personal Use:

I tried to do what you asked, but couldn't.

We tried to climb that wall, but we didn't make it.

We tried something different, but it didn't work.

You wanted me to try to come up with a new invention. I couldn't come up with anything, but I did try.

I tried using my new computer, but it made me so mad, I quit.

SETTING US UP TO FAIL

When you were young, you were probably told at one time or another to try something — food, a chore, or homework — by parents/guardians or other authority figures. You were most likely assured that if you didn't like it or couldn't do it, then *it was okay, as long as you tried.*

Hearing this often enough reinforced the idea that it's okay if you don't succeed, as long as you tried. There were no consequences if you failed, and you figured out it was easier to "try" than to actually succeed.

Each time you said, "I couldn't do it, but I tried." Your parents reinforced your belief that trying was all that was necessary. So, as you approached adulthood, you've learned is that all you need to get by is to try, and you never worry about actually succeeding at anything difficult you do. Trying has become the new definition of failure.

IMPLIED FAILURE

The point is that when we say we are trying we don't really have to actually *do* anything. Saying this provides us with an excuse for why we didn't accomplish what we set out to do.

Do you understand the difference? You either do something or you don't do it. Trying is really the same as not doing it. It just makes it easier for us to let ourselves off the hook when we fail.

Where are you trying to improve?

Are you trying to get in shape—or are you getting in shape?

Are you trying to improve your marriage—or are improving your marriage?

Are you trying to make more sales calls—or are you making more sales calls?

This may sound like a small distinction, but it has huge ramifications. If you do not make the intellectual transformation away from the concept that merely trying without succeeding is okay, then failure will become the acceptable result for everything you do in your adult life. While your childhood may have reinforced this thinking, you have to break the habit of trying to do something and replace it with a habit of successfully completing what you set out to do.

> *You do not have the right to quit trying. The universe wobbles when you do.*
>
> ~ DR. SUNWOLF

You must also be aware that when you use the word try when asking people to do things, you are implying that you will be satisfied if the task is not completed. You can help others out of the trying mind-set by clearly stating you want the job done completely and as quickly as possible.

Words matter, and we should pay attention to the way we phrase things so that our implied meaning is what we actually mean to say. For example, if a parents or guardian tells their child to "at least try to stay out of trouble." They are sending the wrong message. There should be no "try" to this — the child should stay out of trouble. Period! There should be no ambiguity to these types of statements.

SELF-FULFILLING PROPHECY

Many of the kids use the words try and fail interchangeably; the two words seem to have the same meaning for them. They might say something like, "I've been in trouble most of my life. I try as hard as I can, but I can't stay out of trouble. I'm just a failure."

These same children grow up and use similar wording to describe their failed marriages, inability to stay off drugs/alcohol or to keep a job. They never made the connection between only trying and failure.

Do you acknowledge and accept the fact that you have tried once and failed, then fail to do anything else to try to be successful? This is probably because most of your life you were never expected to finish anything, you just had to try. So rather than trying to do something, say you "will do it" and work at it until you succeed.

The phrase "work at it" implies you will continue until you succeed. By being positive and saying you will do it, then "working at it" until you do, you won't feel like you've failed and will eventually be rewarded by the feeling of success.

If at first you don't succeed, continue to "work on it." You can pass along this wisdom to others in your family and hand it down to your children so they won't be caught in the "trying" and failing cycle you've fought so hard to break.

Remember what Yoda said in *The Empire Strikes Back*, "No. Try not. Do. Or do not. There is no try."

> *Anyone can carry his burden, however hard, until nightfall. Anyone can do his work, however hard, for one day. Anyone can live sweetly, patiently, lovingly, purely, till the sun goes down. And this is all life really means.*
>
> ~ ROBERT LOUIS STEVENSON

CHAPTER 6 QUESTIONS

Try

1. If you "try" hard and cannot succeed, do you think you should keep trying?

   ❏ Yes

   ❏ No

   Explain: _____
   _____

2. Do you "try" harder if the negative consequences increase each time you stop trying?

   ❏ Yes

   ❏ No

   Explain: _____
   _____

3. Do you understand that trying once and then quitting can become a behavior that sets you up for failure as you get older?

   ❏ Yes

   ❏ No

   Explain: _____
   _____

information
REVIEW
train
intelligence
FACT
read
expectations
TEXT
COURSE
STUDENT
Progress
CAREER
Lesson
LEVEL
responsibility
homework
DISCIPLINE
school
test
LEARN
STUDY
FUTURE
Life
THINK
PLAN
college

CHAPTER 7

We Teach People How to Treat Us

In our adult relationships, we are responsible for the way we treat others and for the way we allow others to treat us. It is easy to follow the Golden Rule and treat others as we would like to be treated, and that works, as long as everyone is following the same rule. Problems occur when others mistreat us and we allow it.

We often hear people say that others will treat you the way you treat them. But in reality, people will treat you the way you *teach* them to treat you. We teach each other how we expect to be treated through our behaviors.

For example, do you demand fairness and respect in your relationships, or do you show the other person you will still stay in the relationship even if you're treated badly? Staying when you're being mistreated or abused teaches the other person in the relationship that their behavior toward you is acceptable. Many times, we are shown something similar in childhood by watching how the authority figures and learn through their example — right or wrong. This learned behavior is then passed on to your children, and the problems are perpetuated through the generations.

PARENT FOLLOW THROUGH

Parents hear a lot of talk these days about setting healthy boundaries. Parents everywhere understand the need for rules, the problem for most parents comes with following through.

The danger in making rules and not following through is that children might decide that parents no matter what they do, there's a good chance parents won't follow through with the punishment they've threatened. Believe it or not, one of the ways young children learn trust is when parents provide fair limits with consistent follow through. When parents follow through with dignity and respect, the child knows he can trust them to do what they say they'll do in all instances.

For example, as a parent, you decide to punish your child for bad behavior by saying, "If you do that again there will be no television tonight and you will go straight to bed after dinner." An hour later, the child repeats the behavior and you repeat the consequences. Then when it comes time to enforce the punishment, your child says he must watch a television show and do a report about it for school the next day, so you give in and let her watch television for the rest of the evening. Your child sees that you do not follow through on what

> *While we try to teach our children all about life, Our children teach us what life is all about.*
>
> ~ ANGELA SCHWINDT

you say and this tells her she can continue to push your boundaries without any real consequences. The key to effective limits and boundaries is to say what you mean and mean what you say.

Another example would be your teenager doesn't tell you where she's going and comes home late after school. You tell her there will be serious consequences if she is late again. The problem here is you don't say what the consequences will be. Sometimes we're afraid to be the bad guy and don't want to dole out punishment. We make the mistake of being our child's friend rather than being his parent.

Parents can't have it both ways. Friends don't had out punishments for bad behavior; parents do. Stop being your child's friend and become the parent they need. Teach them respect and fairness and when they grow up, they will insist on the same in their relationships.

> *See everything;*
> *overlook a great deal; correct a little.*
>
> ~ POPE JOHN XXIII

RESPECT FROM OUR PEERS

We start early teaching people how to treat us. When we are teenagers, we want friends and work to be liked by our peers. Sometimes, we let our friends say or do things we don't like or want, just to keep them as friends.

This teaches our friends just how far they can go with teasing or pushing us around. If we like a certain person and want them to like us, we might have almost no limits on how far will we let them go in their poor treatment of us. This can lead to wondering if the person is a friend because they like us or because we let them get away with anything they want.

Even as we get older and start college or join the workforce, we continue to teach people how to treat us, but the stakes are higher now. We must decide what our boundaries and ethics are, and then stick to them.

ROMANTIC RELATIONSHIPS

In romantic relationships we often think of boundaries as a bad thing or simply unnecessary. Isn't our partner supposed to anticipate our wants and needs? Isn't that part of being in love? Aren't boundaries callous? Don't they interfere with the romance and spontaneity of a relationship?

All healthy relationships have boundaries. When the boundary is clearly defined and respected, both people are on equal ground. However, when the boundary is violated in order to do harm or take advantage, then there are problems.

In healthy relationships include taking one another's feelings into account, showing gratitude and respecting differences in opinion. In less healthy relationships, partners assume their partner feels the same way they do without asking, and ignore the effects of violating their partner's boundary.

This is why communicating boundaries and sticking to them is key. Following is an example of failing to set boundaries at the beginning of a relationship.

> *People cannot go wrong, if you don't let them. They cannot go right, unless you let them.*
>
> ~ AUGUSTUS WILLIAM HARE / JULIUS CHARLES HARE

You are dating a new person, and you overlook it when they pick you up late or aren't ready when you arrive to pick them up. You decide to be flexible and accept whatever excuse they give because you want to show them how nice you are. So, you decide to let this behavior slide the first time it happens.

Unfortunately, the next time you have a date, the behavior is repeated. By letting it slide the first time, you taught this person how to treat you. You told them it was okay because you didn't let them know what you expect from them when they've made a commitment to you. Now, you're as much at fault for the situation as they are because they have no way of knowing they've done something wrong.

Letting your expectations be known and expecting the person involved to honor them is not a bad thing. Ultimately, healthy relationships require clear-cut parameters. When couples are clear about the boundaries for their own relationship, that relationship can be stable.

> ## *Dig the well before you are thirsty.*
> ~ CHINESE PROVERB

INTERACTIONS BETWEEN ADULTS

Given that work is such a huge part of most peoples' lives, teaching people how to treat you in this setting should be a big priority. Doing this can lead to being more efficient and confident as well as less stressed.

For example, if you don't want to participate in office gossip because you don't like gossip, then don't sit at lunch and listen to a co-worker gossip about a fellow employee. Politely state your feelings about gossip and ask the person to stop. If they do not, then quietly remove yourself from the situation. Doing this teaches the person you are serious about your beliefs and will follow through.

Here are a few other examples: your coworker consistently takes credit for your ideas or goes out of his way to throw you under the bus, or an adult cousin is always rude to you or takes you for granted. These people are behaving this way toward you because you've taught them you're okay with it. Otherwise, they'd stop.

While you're not responsible for another person's behavior, you have the power to change their behavior. So, if there is a person in your life who isn't treating you with respect and consideration, you have to decide if you're willing to accept accountability, for that treatment. Then ask yourself if you want it to change. If the answer is yes, then you must figure out what you've done to teach them this behavior is acceptable. Even doing nothing is giving them permission to keep up their current behavior. The only person you control is you—you're the one letting her this behavior continue and you're the one who has to put a stop to it.

It's time to take ownership of the role you been play. The payoff when the behavior changes will be well worth it.

CONCLUSION

Don't expect to teach people how to treat you in just one day, or even a week or month — it's going to take some time to consistently get someone to treat you the way you want to be treated. This process takes lots of practice and patience because others can be too caught up in themselves to understand what you're trying to teach them the first time you do it. Persistence and consistency will eventually let you reach your goal.

When you start clarifying what you will and won't tolerate from the people in your life, there's a risk that some of them won't stick around. If this happens, realize that a relationship at the cost of you isn't worth it and move on. The vacancy caused by the person who exited your life is making room for a future relationship you deserve.

CHAPTER 7 QUESTIONS

We Teach People

1. **After dealing with an issue/incident do you often feel you are the one who gave in? Do you wish you could stop doing that and start holding others accountable for their behavior?**

   ❑ Yes

   ❑ No

   Example of what you do now: _____
   _____
   _____
   _____

   If yes, example of what you want to do in the future:
   _____
   _____
   _____
   _____

2. **How often do you threaten consequences for your children's inappropriate behavior, but not follow through on your threatened punishment?**

   ❑ Rarely

   ❑ Sometimes

   ❑ Often

   Explain what you do: _____

   _____

   _____

   _____

   Explain why: _____

   _____

   _____

   _____

3. **As your children grow, do you see them letting their friends get away with things they don't like because they don't want to confront them? Did they learn this behavior from you?**

   ❏ Yes

   ❏ No

   If yes, give an example: _____
   _____
   _____

   If no, why do you think that?:_____
   _____
   _____
   _____

4. **When dating, do/did you have strict boundaries for how you wish to be treated, or do you accept treatment you don't want?**

   ❏ Boundaries

   ❏ Flexibility

   ❏ No Boundaries

   Please explain: _____
   _____
   _____

   Why do you do this? _____
   _____
   _____

5. **Do you expect co-workers and other adults in your life to treat you with respect.**

   ❏ Yes

   ❏ No

   Explain what you expect: _____
   _____
   _____

   Explain what usually happens: _____
   _____
   _____
   _____

   How could you improve this? _____
   _____
   _____
   _____

Author's Note

I hope you found this book beneficial. I tried to cover information that would benefit individuals in a variety of circumstances. The examples I shared were compilations of experiences I've had with clients of all ages over the years. I hope you continue your journey and continue to learn techniques that will help you become the person you want to be. No matter what life has had dealt you up to this point, know that you can make the choice to improve it.

There are very few life settings that cannot be changed by making the right decisions. The first step is deciding what you want to change and then making the commitment to make those changes, one behavior at a time.

Continue to strive to be the best person you can be,
Mike Siver

> *You may believe that you are responsible for what you do, but not for what you think. The truth is that you are responsible for what you think, because it is only at this level that you can exercise choice. What you do comes from what you think.*
>
> ~ MARIANNE WILLIAMSON,
> *A Return to Love: Reflections on the Principles of "A Course in Miracles"*

Sacrifice:

Children should not have to sacrifice so you can have the life you want. You make sacrifices so your children can have the life that they deserve.

Performance Change

There are only two things in the world that motivate people to change behaviors and how they perform in their lives. The explaination below is great for family or group discussions.

There are only two things that influence a person's performance. They are ***Inspiration and Desperation*** or as we more commonly call them ***Pleasure and Pain.***

When you realize this, you can start believing and understanding that ***Pain and Desperation*** will follow if we continue on our current path.

Inspiration motivates you to change your negative behaviors so you can find the ***Pleasure*** and reduce the ***Pain*** in your life.

PARENTING NONVIOLENTLY

The chapters in this book have two main goals:

(1) to help you deal with negative behaviors in your life and

(2) to help you avoid passing those behaviors on to others, including your children, and get you to ask yourself, "Why did I do that?"

In order to break the cycle of irresponsible behaviors, including violence and apathy, we need to change our behaviors so that we teach young people the right message through our actions so they don't perpetuate the cycle.

This book focuses on how we can become better role models for young people, and provide them with more options so they're better equipped to become successful in life.

WHAT IT MEANS TO BE A PARENT

Parenting is more than a biological relationship with children. It means being a caring, helping, nurturing mature member of the community. Caring and nurturing will help to wipe out violence.

Unfortunately, society today encourages us to think primarily of our own needs and survival. Instead, we should be nurturing, active members of our family and community. We can be people for whom there is no higher responsible voice and no one to blame for our problems but ourselves and our actions. When we realize this and take responsibility for our lives, we can give our children alternatives that are non-violent, effective, and healthy.

Parents please don't misunderstand, a parent cannot be a child's friend. As a parent, you are the authority figure and delivery consequences for bad behavior. Friends don't do that. Know what role you play in your child's life.

As a parent, you have a dual authority role. On one side of the coin, you are the trusted figure in your child's life — he or she can come to you with any issue and you will listen and help. On the other side of the coin you are the authority figure who doles out punishment for bad behavior. Your child needs to know that there are consequences if he or she breaks the rules.

SETTING LIMITS FOR CHILDREN

So, you wanted to be a parent and you are. Now, your work really begins. Children endanger themselves occasionally — running into the street, playing with dangerous toys, etc. As a parent, you must respond quickly to dangers and eliminate them, then direct the child to another, safer activity.

When children act willfully defiant, it's important that the parents' level of response equals the level of the defiance. When children exhibit these behaviors there need to be consequences so that the child will be discouraged from repeating the behavior. Some children need to test the boundaries of their environment and may be repeat offenders until they learn the lesson.

This type of behavior needs to be addressed when the children are very young so that they learn the lesson before the behavior becomes something dangerous or violent. Children will test boundaries and do things without an understanding of danger involved. As a parent, you need to teach them the consequences of bad behavior so that as they get older, the lesson will apply to more serious temptations and prevent them from making bad decisions.

Part of the reason children act out is because they're searching for a way to have control over their lives. One way to give them a measure of control is to give them a list of chores to do around the house, and let them choose the three things they will be doing. This way, they will feel they had a choice, rather than just being told what to do. It gives them a little power over their lives, while at the same time learning to look at positive or negative outcomes due to their choices. Another big benefit for parents is the child will soon learn they cannot blame you for their choice.

It is also important that you, as parents, act as role models for your children. Young children don't always have the self-control to stop themselves, so you need to demonstrate your ability to control yourself to show them how it's done. Many times children express their frustration by acting out. Be sure this behavior isn't reinforced by your own actions.

One of the more difficult jobs as a parent is to constantly check to see if we are teaching or enabling our children. At times, it's easy to slip from teaching to being an enabler. Parents should constantly be aware of their own behavior so that their little sponges don't absorb the wrong lessons. Once enabling starts, it's difficult to stop.

Following are some exercises you can complete to see what you learned about parenting when you were a child, and how that may be influencing your parenting style today.

EXERCISE 1
Was hitting, molesting, slapping, spanking, or other physical discipline used in your family when you were a child? If so, how did it affect you and other family members?

_____
_____
_____

EXERCISE 2
Were the children in your family put down, teased, or told negative things like "you're worthless", "you're stupid", "you'll never amount to anything"? If so, how did it affect you and other family members?

_____
_____
_____

Do you feel that you received all the love and encouragement you needed as a child? How was love expressed to you?

_____
_____

EXERCISE 3

Do you want your children to grow up with more love and encouragement than you received? If so, how can you do that without enabling them or being too soft?

> Example: As a parent, your children should believe you will always be there for them and love them no matter what the situation, even when they've misbehaved. You should be sure they know their punishment for misbehaving comes from a place of love and a desire to teach them right from wrong.

_____

_____

_____

EXERCISE 4

It is ok to discipline a child but it is never okay to hit a child. An adult hitting a child is never okay at any time. Is there anything that keeps you from deciding not to hit, tease, call a child names, or otherwise put down young people? If so, describe those barriers here.

_____

_____

_____

_____

EXERCISE 5

When you are tired, frustrated, or angry, what specific things can you do to avoid taking out your frustrations on your children or otherwise abusing them? (For example, can you take an adult time out.) You would be surprised; this is the times when timeout really works.

_____
_____
_____
_____

EXERCISE 6

List ways to set boundaries with children and young people that do not involve violence. Which options are you going to use and why?

_____
_____
_____
_____
_____
_____

EXERCISE 7

What rules for respect and cooperative living do you think your family needs to establish?

_____
_____
_____
_____

EXERCISE 8

What are ways for family members to express anger, hurt, and frustration without violence? (Learn to recognize frustration and that frustration is the first stage of anger.)

_____
_____
_____
_____

EXERCISE 9

How can you empower your children to stand up for themselves and teach them to ask for help when they need it? Be specific, and think if each of child's individual needs.

_____
_____
_____
_____

EXERCISE 10

What steps can you take to introduce respect, the willingness to listen, and not taking others for granted?

> (Example: At the family dinner you could ask each family member to explain a good thing they did or had happen to them and then ask them to explain something that may have been not so good and talk about how they felt about it).)

_____
_____
_____
_____
_____

EXERCISE 11

If you have daughters, how can you encourage them to be adventurous, independent, and confident that they'll succeed in whatever they undertake, while at the same time setting boundaries, and ensuring she respects the family and obeys house rules?

_____

_____

_____

_____

_____

EXERCISE 12

If you have sons, how can you help them to resist the pressures to be insensitive and overly tough and aggressive? How can you teach them to respect women and to treat women as equals?

_____

_____

_____

_____

_____

EXERCISE 13

Think of yourself and your children as peacemakers and conflict resolvers. Is this hard to do? If so, why? If not, why not? What specific steps can you take to give you and your children skills in resolving conflict?

_____

_____

_____

_____

_____

_____

_____

GUMBO

This acronym is a great for everyone to grow up with. If we all learned it at a very young age, we may have taken more time to understand what we were doing or wanted to do to give us all the opportunities in life

Greater
Understanding
Means
Better
Opportunities

FINGERTIP GOALS

- Have 10-12 participants stand in a circle, each person is to set a very simple individual goal that they are able to accomplish in a relatively short period of time within the confines of the room and at this time keep the goal to themselves.

- Next have all members participating join their pinky fingers together with the person next to them until the circle is inter-connected.

- Now have each participant tell the rest of the group what their individual goal is.

- After that is completed, explain to the group they must all complete their goals and may not let go of the fingers they are attached to.

After completion of the exercise, have the group or family discuss the exercise as a metaphor for group and or family dynamics. Although some of the goals could have been completed on there own, it shows how at times it is work to include everyone, but the end result in most cases is more fun and if thought out as a group the individual goals completed collectively can be done faster leaving more time for growth or family fun.

This section is for those who feel the need after they have read the book to see how they rate if they become overwhelmed with new knowledge that they may have to change their behaviors and are struggling with it to the point of some depression.

CES-D Test for Depression

The Center for Epidemiologic Studies Depression Scale (CES-D) was originally developed by Lenore Radloff of Utah State University. The quick self-test measures depressive feelings and behaviors during the past week.

1. I was bothered by things that don't usually bother me.

❑ Rarely or none of the time (<1 day)

❑ Some or a little of the time (1-2 days)

❑ Occasionally or a moderate amount of the time (3-4 days)

❑ Most or all of the time (5-7 days)

2. I did not feel like eating; my appetite was poor.

❑ Rarely or none of the time (<1 day)

❑ Some or a little of the time (1-2 days)

❑ Occasionally or a moderate amount of the time (3-4 days)

❑ Most or all of the time (5-7 days)

3. **I felt that I could not shake off the blues even with the help of my family or friends.**

☐ Rarely or none of the time (<1 day)

☐ Some or a little of the time (1-2 days)

☐ Occasionally or a moderate amount of the time (3-4 days)

☐ Most or all of the time (5-7 days)

4. **I felt that I was just as good as other people.**

☐ Rarely or none of the time (<1 day)

☐ Some or a little of the time (1-2 days)

☐ Occasionally or a moderate amount of the time (3-4 days)

☐ Most or all of the time (5-7 days)

5. **I had trouble keeping my mind on what I was doing.**

☐ Rarely or none of the time (<1 day)

☐ Some or a little of the time (1-2 days)

☐ Occasionally or a moderate amount of the time (3-4 days)

☐ Most or all of the time (5-7 days)

6. I felt depressed.

❏ Rarely or none of the time (<1 day)

❏ Some or a little of the time (1-2 days)

❏ Occasionally or a moderate amount of the time (3-4 days)

❏ Most or all of the time (5-7 days)

7. I felt everything I did was an effort.

❏ Rarely or none of the time (<1 day)

❏ Some or a little of the time (1-2 days)

❏ Occasionally or a moderate amount of the time (3-4 days)

❏ Most or all of the time (5-7 days)

8. I felt hopeful about the future.

❏ Rarely or none of the time (<1 day)

❏ Some or a little of the time (1-2 days)

❏ Occasionally or a moderate amount of the time (3-4 days)

❏ Most or all of the time (5-7 days)

9. I thought my life had been a failure.

❑ Rarely or none of the time (<1 day)

❑ Some or a little of the time (1-2 days)

❑ Occasionally or a moderate amount of the time (3-4 days)

❑ Most or all of the time (5-7 days)

10. I felt fearful.

❑ Rarely or none of the time (<1 day)

❑ Some or a little of the time (1-2 days)

❑ Occasionally or a moderate amount of the time (3-4 days)

❑ Most or all of the time (5-7 days)

11. My sleep was restless.

❑ Rarely or none of the time (<1 day)

❑ Some or a little of the time (1-2 days)

❑ Occasionally or a moderate amount of the time (3-4 days)

❑ Most or all of the time (5-7 days)

12. I was happy.

❏ Rarely or none of the time (<1 day)

❏ Some or a little of the time (1-2 days)

❏ Occasionally or a moderate amount of the time (3-4 days)

❏ Most or all of the time (5-7 days)

13. I talked less than usual.

❏ Rarely or none of the time (<1 day)

❏ Some or a little of the time (1-2 days)

❏ Occasionally or a moderate amount of the time (3-4 days)

❏ Most or all of the time (5-7 days)

14. I felt lonely.

❏ Rarely or none of the time (<1 day)

❏ Some or a little of the time (1-2 days)

❏ Occasionally or a moderate amount of the time (3-4 days)

❏ Most or all of the time (5-7 days)

15. People were unfriendly.

❑ Rarely or none of the time (<1 day)

❑ Some or a little of the time (1-2 days)

❑ Occasionally or a moderate amount of the time (3-4 days)

❑ Most or all of the time (5-7 days)

16. I enjoyed life.

❑ Rarely or none of the time (<1 day)

❑ Some or a little of the time (1-2 days)

❑ Occasionally or a moderate amount of the time (3-4 days)

❑ Most or all of the time (5-7 days)

17. I had crying spells.

❑ Rarely or none of the time (<1 day)

❑ Some or a little of the time (1-2 days)

❑ Occasionally or a moderate amount of the time (3-4 days)

❑ Most or all of the time (5-7 days)

18. I felt sad.

❏ Rarely or none of the time (<1 day)

❏ Some or a little of the time (1-2 days)

❏ Occasionally or a moderate amount of the time (3-4 days)

❏ Most or all of the time (5-7 days)

19. I felt that people disliked me.

❏ Rarely or none of the time (<1 day)

❏ Some or a little of the time (1-2 days)

❏ Occasionally or a moderate amount of the time (3-4 days)

❏ Most or all of the time (5-7 days)

20. I could not get "going".

❏ Rarely or none of the time (<1 day)

❏ Some or a little of the time (1-2 days)

❏ Occasionally or a moderate amount of the time (3-4 days)

❏ Most or all of the time (5-7 days)

ABOUT SCORING THIS PSYCHOLOGICAL QUESTIONNAIRE

Scoring for All Except Questions 4, 8, 12, and 16:

0 points — Rarely or none of the time (< 1 day)
1 point — Some or a little of the time (1-2 days)
2 points — Occasionally or a moderate amount of the time (3-4 days)
3 points — Most or all of the time (5-7 days)

Scoring for 4, 8, 12, and 16:

3 points — Rarely or none of the time (< 1 day)
2 point — Some or a little of the time (1-2 days)
1 points — Occasionally or a moderate amount of the time (3-4 days)
0 points — Most or all of the time (5-7 days)

Screening test scoring ranges:

Less than 15 — Not Depressed
15-21 — Mild to Moderate Depression
Over 21 — Possibility of Major Depression

Depression Test Results Considerations

After you have taken the test and answered the question honestly and truthfully and are now taking time to digest the results, you may even have more questions. Many times it takes a professional to help go over some of the things these test expose in us. It may now be appropriate to contact a Psychologist or Psychiatrist, explain to them the test you have taken and that you have questions. The professional should be able to help you put your questions in perspective and if something needs to be addressed prioritize the process.

About the Authors

Mike is a Master Addiction Counselor, Certified Domestic Violence Counselor and a Board Certified Biblical Counselor. Before retiring, he provided Anger Management, Domestic Violence, Substance Abuse counseling and assessments for Van Buren County and Blue Seahorse. Inc., a non-profit (501c3) community-based organization.

He worked with Van Buren County Family Services for placement of mothers and children from family of domestic violence situations and is a Chaplain for Forgotten Man Ministries.

April Siver was born in Michigan, the fourth of seven children. She received her public education in Southwest Michigan, her bachelor's degree at East Tennessee State University, and her master's degree at UNT in Denton, TX. She has worked in public education for 27 years. April has two daughters and four grandchildren, and resides in North Texas where she currently teaches high school. April also works as educational director for the nonprofit corporation, No Fences, Inc. where she uses her knowledge and skills to provide a helping hand to others through mentoring and tutoring.

April chose to co-author this book because she believes it to be a powerful tool for the No Fences program, as well as other individuals and organizations working to help people of all ages live the best life possible. It is her belief that no matter how hopeless things may appear, there is always a way to knock down any "FENCES" we may have in our way to turn things around. The trick is to keep trying.